DISCARD

Greatest RIVALRIES in Sports

by

Published by ABDO Publishing Company, PO Box 398166, Minneapolis, MN 55439. Copyright © 2014 by Abdo Consulting Group, Inc. International copyrights reserved in all countries. No part of this book may be reproduced in any form without written permission from the publisher. SportsZone™ is a trademark and logo of ABDO Publishing Company.

Printed in the United States of America,
North Mankato, Minnesota
052013
092013

 THIS BOOK CONTAINS AT LEAST 10% RECYCLED MATERIALS.

Editor: Chrös McDougall
Series Designer: Craig Hinton

Photo Credits: Scott Boehm/AP Images, cover, 1; The Plain Dealer/Chuck Crow/AP Images, 5, 7; Tuscaloosa News/Robert Sutton/AP Images, 9; Bill Nichols/AP Images, 11; Aaron M. Sprecher/AP Images, 13; David Drapkin/AP Images, 14; Mark Lennihan/AP Images, 17; Abe Fox/AP Images, 18; AP Images, 21, 51, 54, 58; Tom Gannam/AP Images, 23; Rick Stewart/Allsport/Getty Images, 25; Winslow Townson/AP Images, 27; Gerry Broome/AP Images, 29; Bob Child/AP Images, 33; The Canadian Press/Ryan Remiorz/AP Images, 35; Cal Sport Media via AP Images, 37; Denis Paquin/AP Images, 40; Manu Fernandez/AP Images, 43; Press Association via AP Images, 45, 52; Elsa Hasch / Allsport/AP Images, 47; Ibrahim Usta/AP Images, 49; Dave Caulkin/AP Images, 57

Library of Congress Control Number: 2013932588

Cataloging-in-Publication Data
Lee, Tony.
 Greatest rivalries in sports / Tony Lee.
  p. cm. -- (Sports' biggest moments)
ISBN 978-1-61783-925-2
Includes bibliographical references and index.
1. Sports rivalries--Juvenile literature. 2. Sports--Miscellanea--Juvenile literature. I. Title.
796--dc23

                                                            2013932588

TABLE OF CONTENTS

Chapter 1

GREAT FOOTBALL RIVALRIES

Their campuses are separated by less than 200 miles (322 km). They have played football since 1897. For many who live in these states, few things matter more than the Ohio State University Buckeyes vs. University of Michigan Wolverines football game.

Since 1935, this game has been the last one on each team's regular-season schedule. It often decides the Big Ten Conference title. Sometimes it determines if one team goes on to play for the national championship. But the rivalry goes far beyond wins and losses.

A Michigan alumnus will argue that Michigan Stadium is the greatest place on earth. With seating for 109,901, "The Big House" is the biggest football stadium in the United States. But to Ohio State fans, Ohio Stadium is at the center of college football. The stadium nicknamed "The Horseshoe" is one of the sport's most famous, as well.

An Ohio State fan (*in red*) cheers while a Michigan fan boos during a game at Ohio State.

After Navy defeated Army in 2012, many watched on TV as Army senior quarterback Trent Steelman cried. He had just lost to the Midshipmen for the fourth straight time. It showed in his face, filled with tears, how important this game is to those who play it. These teams were college football powerhouses in the 1940s and 1950s. They battled it out with the University of Notre Dame, the University of Michigan, and others for the top of the rankings. Army won three national titles. Both schools had multiple Heisman Trophy winners. In the end, the rivalry is filled with respect. Both are institutions that educate and train national leaders.

There have been many memorable games over the years. Older fans might remember the "Snow Bowl" of 1950. After a blizzard hit Columbus, Ohio, the Buckeyes were told that they could cancel the game. If so, they would still get the win and would take home the conference championship. Ohio State chose to play the game in awful conditions, but lost 9–3. All of Michigan's points came on blocked punts. The Wolverines, not the Buckeyes, went to the Rose Bowl.

Woody Hayes took over as Ohio State's coach after that controversial game. Several other big games came when Hayes and Michigan coach Bo Schembechler met from 1969 to 1978. That period became known as "The Ten Year War." Perhaps no rivalry has ever been as intense as this one was during those years.

In 1969, Michigan defeated top-ranked Ohio State in one of the biggest upsets of the rivalry. From 1970 to 1975, the Wolverines entered this game without a loss each time. They won just once.

Football games between Ohio State and Michigan are almost always competitive and intense.

In the 1990s, Michigan returned the favor. The Buckeyes were unbeaten three times heading into the game. Each time, the Wolverines pulled off the upset. In 2006, the day after Schembechler died, top-ranked Ohio State defeated second-ranked Michigan 42–39.

Many of these games mean so much to all of college football. Even when they don't, they always matter to those in Ohio and Michigan.

The Iron Bowl

The Iron Bowl does not have the longevity of the Michigan-Ohio State rivalry. The annual games between the University of Alabama Crimson Tide and the Auburn University Tigers do not lack passion or intensity, though.

The bitterness between the two Alabama schools actually began off the football field. In fact, these two schools did not even play for 40 years because of a minor disagreement back in 1908.

Auburn wanted to provide the official for the game that year. So did Alabama. Auburn wanted its players to be fed if they made the trip to Alabama's campus in Tuscaloosa. The Crimson Tide did not want to pay for the food. The game was cancelled. Both sides held a grudge for decades. They finally began play again in 1948. Even then, however, the state government had to step in to help settle the dispute.

IVY LEAGUERS

These days, Harvard University and Yale University are most known for their academics. Yet on the gridiron, these two Ivy League schools were two of the first powers. The Crimson and Bulldogs have met almost every year since 1875. To fans the contest is known simply as "The Game." Some meetings, like in 1894, were violent. In that game, one player broke a leg. Others had their eyes gouged, and one was left in a coma. Another memorable game came in 1968. Both teams were 8-0. Yale led by 16 points in the final minute. Many fans left. Amazingly, the Crimson tied it. It almost felt like a win. The famous headline in a Harvard newspaper read, "Harvard Beats Yale, 29–29."

More than 100,000 fans at Bryant-Denny Stadium on the University of Alabama campus cheer at the 2008 Iron Bowl.

Eventually, the Iron Bowl became as bitter a feud as any in college football. It was played for many years on a neutral field in Birmingham, Alabama. Tickets were split between both schools. After approximately 50 years that setup finally changed in the 1990s. Today the game rotates between Alabama's and Auburn's home stadiums.

Alabama is one of the most successful programs in college football history. The Iron Bowl, however, has been fairly even over the years. There have been exceptions, though. Auburn fans will always curse Bear Bryant. The legendary Alabama coach led his team to wins in 19 of 25 games against the Tigers. Crimson Tide supporters still grimace when someone mentions Tigers running back Bo Jackson. His leap over the line for a late touchdown gave Auburn a win in Bryant's last regular-season game in 1982. Bryant died two months later. Jackson ran for an Iron Bowl-record 256 yards the next year as the Tigers won again.

Perhaps the most famous Iron Bowl was in 1972. Both teams came into the game with one loss. Alabama led 16–0 in the fourth quarter. Then Auburn returned two blocked punts for touchdowns and won 17–16. The game became known as "Punt Bama Punt."

Black and Blue (and Bitter Cold)

When the National Football League (NFL) debuted in 1920, there was no *Monday Night Football*, no 32-team league, and definitely no Super Bowl. The Chicago Bears—then called the Decatur Staleys—were there, though. And one year later, the Green Bay Packers were there, too. Ever since, the two teams have been the league's most bitter rivals.

As the NFL grew, the Bears and Packers formed the heart of the National Football Conference (NFC) Central Division. It became known as the "Black and Blue Division." The games between the Bears, Packers, Detroit Lions, and Minnesota Vikings were often brutal. They were often fought in freezing cold weather, too. While some cold-weather teams have moved indoors, the Bears and Packers still play home games outside.

George "Papa Bear" Halas was one of the NFL's founding fathers. He coached the Bears for 40 years. Halas actually helped the Packers get their feet off the ground with some financial help in the 1920s.

The Chicago Bears and Green Bay Packers met outside in Chicago on January 23, 2011, to determine which team went to the Super Bowl.

Since then, Green Bay had won 13 titles through 2012. That was more than any other team. Second on that list was Chicago with nine. These teams also had more Hall of Famers than anyone else. Among them are greats such as Packers quarterback Bart Starr and legendary coach Vince Lombardi. From the Bears, superstar running back Walter Payton and

Just one look at the Cotton Bowl in Dallas each year says it all. The crowd is split at the 50-yard line. On one side are University of Texas Longhorns fans in burnt orange. The other half is dressed in University of Oklahoma Sooners crimson. Known as the "Red River Rivalry," this game has been played since 1900. The Longhorns see the Sooners as country folk. Oklahoma sees Texas as a snobby school. Those feelings fuel the rivalry, which is almost always a huge game nationally. The teams combined for 10 national titles through 2012.

linebacker Dick Butkus headline the list. Also, the series has been very even. Through 2012, Chicago had won 92 meetings. Green Bay had won 88. There were six ties.

Despite their long histories, the teams have met only twice in the playoffs through 2012. The first came in 1941, when the Bears won at Wrigley Field in Chicago. The next came in the 2010 NFC Championship Game. Green Bay triumphed at Soldier Field in Chicago and went on to win its fourth Super Bowl.

Fans of both teams will never forget defensive lineman William "The Refrigerator" Perry scoring his first career touchdown as a running back against the Packers on *Monday Night Football* in 1985. Before an intense rematch a few weeks later, Green Bay players put manure in Chicago's locker room. A year later, Packers defensive lineman Charles Martin slammed Bears quarterback Jim McMahon to the turf after the

The Red River Rivalry between Oklahoma and Texas is held each year during the Texas State Fair in Dallas.

whistle. McMahon was out for the year. It is one of the lasting images of a violent feud.

When teams win the NFC, they get the Halas Trophy. If they win the Super Bowl, they get the Lombardi Trophy. That says it all about the NFL's oldest rivalry.

Cowboys-Redskins

More than 1,100 miles (1,770 km) separate Dallas and Washington DC. Yet when the NFL made new divisions in 2002, the league made sure the

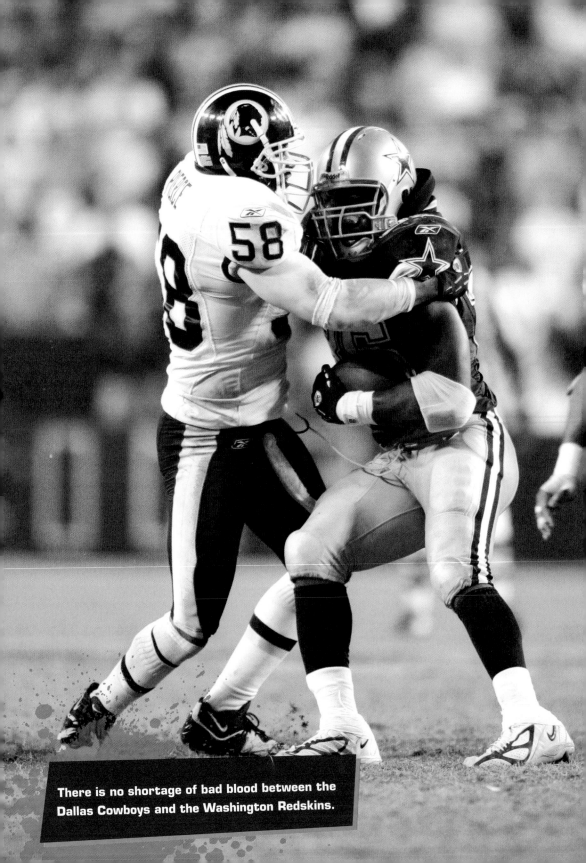

There is no shortage of bad blood between the
Dallas Cowboys and the Washington Redskins.

Dallas Cowboys and Washington Redskins stayed together in the NFC East. After all, they have played in the same division since 1961. And they have hated each other the entire time.

That hatred grew in the 1970s. Dallas president and general manager Tex Schramm and Washington coach George Allen often took shots at each other through the media. Another of Allen's favorite targets was Cowboys Hall of Fame quarterback Roger Staubach. Schramm once accused longtime Washington kicker Mark Moseley of wearing illegal cleats. He even watched the kicker during pregame warm-ups to try to catch him cheating.

Among the more memorable games was the 1974 meeting on Thanksgiving. Washington took a 16–3 lead in the third quarter. Then Dallas slowly began coming back. Still, the game appeared over when Dallas got the ball back with 1:45 to play and down 23–17. Then backup rookie quarterback Clint Longley, in his first regular-season game, replaced an injured Staubach and became the hero. He threw a 50-yard touchdown pass to Drew Pearson with 28 seconds left. That gave Dallas a 24–23 win. Allen said it was "probably the toughest loss we ever had."

Maybe so. Their most embarrassing loss might have been in 1989. That's when the Cowboys were 1–15 but got their only win against the Redskins. In Washington.

Chapter 2

GREAT BASEBALL RIVALRIES

There was a time when the Boston Red Sox dominated the American League (AL). They won five World Series between 1903 and 1918. Then they sold Babe Ruth to the New York Yankees.

For most of the next six decades, the Yankees were the top team in baseball. In fact, from the time Ruth swapped cities through 2000, the Yankees won 26 World Series titles. The Red Sox had none. As such, Red Sox fans grew to dislike the Yankees more and more every year.

Many older fans will remember the great pennant races between the two in 1948 and 1949. The next generation will recall Bucky Dent. The Yankees and Red Sox were tied atop their division at the end of the 1978 regular season. So they met for one extra game to determine the division winner. Dent was hardly a power hitter. Yet his home run in Fenway Park ended the Red Sox's season on a sour note—again.

A New York Yankees fan in 2002 reminded the Boston Red Sox when they won their last World Series—1918.

Boston's Ted Williams, *left*, and the Yankees' Joe DiMaggio were the faces of their teams for much of the 1940s.

Newcomers to the rivalry tell stories of the 2003 AL Championship Series. New York won it in seven memorable games. During one of those games, Boston ace Pedro Martinez threw Yankees bench coach Don Zimmer to the ground in a wild fight.

Their 2004 AL Championship Series was even more famous. That series looked like a blowout early on. New York won the first three games. Then Boston did what no team had done before and won the next four

TEDDY BALLGAME AND JOLTIN' JOE

The Yankees-Red Sox rivalry was special for many reasons. For many years, the two main reasons were Ted Williams and Joe DiMaggio. Both players missed seasons in their primes while serving in the military. But Williams was the Red Sox's left fielder for most seasons from 1939 to 1960. He was perhaps the best hitter in baseball history. DiMaggio played center field for the Yankees for most seasons between 1936 to 1951. He was one of the game's best all-around players. For years, fans debated who was better.

Williams was loud, brash, and hated to dress up. DiMaggio was quiet, serious, and wore suits. They were opposites everywhere except on the field, especially in 1941. That was when Williams hit .406 and DiMaggio had a 56-game hitting streak. Through 2012, nobody has matched those numbers.

games. That sent the Red Sox to the World Series. With a four-game sweep of the St. Louis Cardinals, Boston had its first World Series title since 1918.

Red Sox fans called it the greatest comeback in sports history. Or, if they wanted to insult the hated Yankees, they called it the biggest choke in sports history.

Throughout this rivalry, there have been many fights. In 1938, Red Sox great Joe Cronin was involved in a brawl on the field. Later several Yankees players attacked him in a tunnel behind the dugout. Hall of Fame catcher Carlton Fisk got in several fights with Yankees during the 1970s. The Martinez-Zimmer encounter will never be forgotten. Neither will the time Red Sox catcher Jason Varitek and Yankees third baseman Alex Rodriguez fought at Boston's Fenway Park in 2004.

It was all part of what many consider to be the best rivalry in all of sports.

Rivals on Both Coasts

Rivalries are often based on history, tradition, and geography. The Dodgers-Giants rivalry took those things to a new level. The Giants began in 1883 in New York. The Dodgers were founded one year later in Brooklyn. Long before the Mets and even before the Yankees, these two National League (NL) teams represented New York City. They battled for pennants in ballparks that were just a few miles apart from each other.

Everything changed in 1958. Major League Baseball (MLB) did not have any teams on the West Coast. So the two New York rivals packed up and headed to California. The Dodgers went south to Los Angeles. The Giants went north to San Francisco. Their ballparks were no longer in the same city. But their rivalry continued—with totally new fans. The Dodgers-Giants rivalry is MLB's biggest on the West Coast.

The most famous game in the rivalry came in the New York years. Baseball did not have playoffs outside of the World Series for many years.

YANKEES-DODGERS

From 1941 to 1956, the New York Yankees and Brooklyn Dodgers met in the World Series seven times. With Yankee Stadium and Ebbets Field separated by just a few miles, it turned the city of New York into a baseball party almost every October. The Yankees often won. However, the Dodgers beat New York in 1955 and again in 1963 after moving to Los Angeles. Through 2012, the teams had met 11 times in the World Series, more than any other pair of teams. Through the years, some of the most famous players in baseball history have taken part in this rivalry. Among them are Yogi Berra, Roy Campanella, Mickey Mantle, Duke Snider, Joe DiMaggio, and Jackie Robinson.

New York Giants slugger Bobby Thomson reaches home plate after his pennant-clinching home run in 1951.

But the Giants and Dodgers tied for the NL title in 1951, so they met for a three-game series to determine who won the NL pennant. It was an anticipated series. And when the Giants' Bobby Thomson hit the series-winning walk-off homer, the radio announcer went crazy. The hit became known as the "Shot Heard 'Round the World."

The two teams have played many memorable games on the West Coast, too. In 1962, the teams again tied for the league title. Once again, however, the Giants won in a three-game playoff. A few years later, playoffs became the norm when the AL and NL Championship Series debuted.

College baseball has many great rivalries, but none surpass the passion of the in-state feud between the Clemson University Tigers and the University of South Carolina Gamecocks. College sports are a big deal in South Carolina. That is in part because there are no major professional sports teams there. So this annual battle becomes the focus of the entire Palmetto State. The Tigers and Gamecocks have played baseball since 1899. The rivalry intensified in recent years as they met twice in the semifinals of the College World Series. South Carolina won both times. The Gamecocks won a national title after getting past Clemson in 2010.

Cardinals-Cubs

On summer days in the Midwest, sports fans in Chicago and St. Louis dream of ball games between the Cubs and Cardinals. The results are not always even. The Cardinals won 11 World Series between 1926 and 2012. The Cubs have had so much bad luck that many consider them cursed. Their last World Series victory was in 1908. They have gone longer than any team in baseball since their last title.

But the two teams from baseball-crazed cities have some of the most passionate fans. Win or lose, fans at Wrigley Field in Chicago are among the most loyal in sports. Down in St. Louis, Cardinals fans are often called the best in baseball.

The Cards have been the better team, but the Cubs have had their moments. In a very famous 1984 game on national TV, future Hall of Famer Ryne Sandberg hit game-tying home runs in the ninth and 10th innings. Chicago won 12–11 in 11 innings.

The Cubs also claim legendary broadcaster Harry Caray as their own. He broadcast Cardinals games for more than 20 years but was fired in

St. Louis Cardinals fans cheer after their team beat the Chicago Cubs with a walk-off grand slam in 2006.

1969. He came to Chicago to do White Sox games in 1971 and moved across town in 1982. Caray became a famous supporter of the Cubs.

That helped Chicago fans get over the Lou Brock trade. Brock was traded from the Cubs to the Cardinals in 1964. He became a Hall of Famer. The players Chicago picked up did very little. It is considered one of the most lopsided trades in baseball history.

Chapter 3

GREAT BASKETBALL RIVALRIES

One team played in a cramped, dark gym in a working-class section of Boston. The other played in a shiny arena filled with Hollywood stars. Quite often, they met in the National Basketball Association (NBA) Finals.

In fact, the Boston Celtics and Los Angeles Lakers faced off for the big prize six times in the 1960s, three more times in the 1980s, and again in 2008 and 2010. Both teams eventually moved into shiny new arenas. But through the years one thing stayed the same: This rivalry featured some of the NBA's greatest one-on-one matchups.

Bill Russell vs. Wilt Chamberlain and John Havlicek vs. Elgin Baylor in the 1960s. Larry Bird vs. Earvin "Magic" Johnson in the 1980s. Paul Pierce vs. Kobe Bryant in 2008 and 2010. Many of the best players in NBA history have faced off in this fierce rivalry.

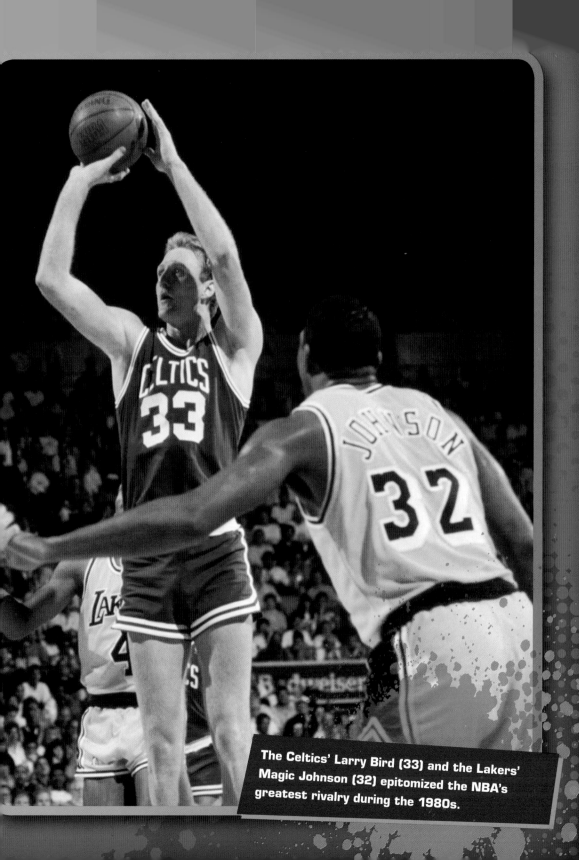

The Celtics' Larry Bird (33) and the Lakers' Magic Johnson (32) epitomized the NBA's greatest rivalry during the 1980s.

MAGIC AND BIRD

Both were Midwestern boys. Both were listed at 6-foot-9. Both were intense competitors. Those were the similarities when Magic Johnson and Larry Bird took the NBA by storm in the 1980s. They also had big differences. Johnson was black and led the flashy Showtime Lakers on the West Coast. Bird was white and the gritty leader of the blue-collar Celtics on the East Coast. They were the perfect pair and the greatest rivals at the same time. From 1980 to 1990, Bird and Johnson won a combined total of eight NBA titles and six Most Valuable Player (MVP) Awards.

The Celtics and Lakers have traditionally been the NBA's best teams. Through 2012, only the Celtics with 17 had more championships than the Lakers' 16. Including the Lakers' time in Minneapolis, the two teams had met 12 times in the NBA Finals. Among the great encounters was 1969.

The Celtics were the NBA's superpower. Russell had led the team to 10 championships in the previous 12 seasons. Six of those wins came over the Lakers. The rematch in 1969 looked like it might finally be the Lakers' chance to win. Chamberlain had joined the team that year. Meanwhile, Russell was in his last season, and the Celtics were getting old. But Russell and the Celtics frustrated the Lakers once again. Boston won in a seven-game series.

The rivalry took a big step in the 1980s. The two teams were again atop the NBA. And the Celtics' Bird and the Lakers' Johnson were far and away the league's most popular players. They met for the first time in the

The Celtics' Paul Pierce and the Lakers' Kobe Bryant rejuvenated the rivalry in the 2000s.

NBA Finals in 1984. The Celtics hosted Game 5. But Boston was in a heat wave. The Boston Garden did not have air conditioning. It was 97 degrees inside the building when the game started. That was no problem for Bird. He scored 34 points. Boston won easily as the Lakers put on oxygen masks on the sidelines. The Celtics went on to win the series.

Los Angeles got its revenge in 1985 and then again in 1987. In 1987, Johnson hit a famous "Baby Hook" to win Game 4 in the Garden. All told the two teams combined to win eight of the nine NBA titles between 1980 and 1988. Many credit their rivalry in that decade for making the NBA as popular as it is today.

Tobacco Road

The Duke University Blue Devils and University of North Carolina Tar Heels are two of the most storied college basketball programs ever. Their campuses are just 8 miles (12.8 km) apart in an area known as Tobacco Road.

Duke's Cameron Crazies cheer on the Blue Devils prior to a 2013 game against North Carolina.

GEORGETOWN–SYRACUSE

The Big East Conference was founded in 1979. The Georgetown University Hoyas and Syracuse University Orange became major forces on the national scene soon after. The rivalry truly began in 1980. That year Syracuse had a 57-game winning streak at home in Manley Field House. Georgetown ended it. After the upset, Hoyas coach John Thompson declared that Manley Field House was "officially closed." It was a comment that rattled Orange fans. It set the stage for years of physical, close battles that often helped decide the Big East.

North Carolina is the public school of Michael Jordan and powder blue uniforms. Duke is the private school where coach Mike Krzyzewski reigns over his royal blue-clad team in the famous Cameron Indoor Stadium. Both schools are known for having some of the most passionate fans in college basketball. And with such close campuses, fans from each school can't help but run into one another. As Krzyzewski once said about the two sides, "We share the same dry cleaners."

Put all of that together and it is a recipe for the greatest rivalry in men's college basketball. Both teams are routinely in the mix for national championships. Yet it's the fans that truly set this rivalry apart. They are so passionate. The Cameron Crazies at Duke are known for filling up their small stadium with energy and clever cheers. The loud North Carolina fans make the Dean Smith Center one of the hardest places for opponents to win.

Both sides have had a lot to cheer about. From 1982 to 2010 they combined to win eight of 29 national titles. Almost every Atlantic Coast Conference championship went to either the Tar Heels or Blue Devils over these years.

And some of the most famous college basketball players ever have suited up in powder blue or royal blue. Jordan, Vince Carter, and Tyler Hansbrough are among the North Carolina greats. Christian Laettner, Shane Battier, and Kyle Singler have starred for Duke. It's no wonder fans often camp out for days just to get tickets to see these two rivals play.

Connecticut-Tennessee

Women's basketball hardly existed in the early 1970s. A government action called Title IX in 1972 changed that. It required schools to offer equal opportunities to men and women. Women's college basketball steadily grew after that. It took off in the 1990s. Much of that was credited to the rivalry between the sport's iconic teams: the University of Connecticut Huskies and the University of Tennessee Lady Volunteers.

Pat Summitt's Lady Vols were at the top of the sport in the 1980s. They won the national title in 1987 and 1989. But Connecticut was building something special under coach Geno Auriemma.

Pretty soon it was hard to keep these teams apart. They played during the regular season every year from 1995 to 2007. They also met seven times in the National Collegiate Athletic Association Tournament. Four of those games decided the title. Connecticut won all four. Tennessee won an overtime game in the semifinals in 1996 that brought the rivalry to another level.

Many of the greatest women's basketball players from that time suited up in either Tennessee orange or Connecticut blue. Lady Vols fans will always remember stars such as Chamique Holdsclaw and Candace Parker. Rebecca Lobo, Sue Bird, and Diana Taurasi are legends in Connecticut.

Summitt and Auriemma were never shy about going after each other. They even had a war of words after the annual series ended. Although the series stopped, the great players and games that were part of this dramatic rivalry helped make women's basketball what it is today.

Connecticut's Diana Taurasi celebrates after her team beat Tennessee in the 2003 Final Four.

Chapter 4

GREAT HOCKEY RIVALRIES

The Stanley Cup has been around since the nineteenth century. To most people, however, modern hockey began in 1942. The National Hockey League (NHL) cut back to six teams in 1942–43. Those "Original Six" teams were the only six teams in the league for the next 25 seasons. That resulted in some incredible rivalries.

No NHL rivalry brought out more emotion than that of the Boston Bruins and Montreal Canadiens. In the early years, it was very one-sided. Montreal won 18 straight playoff series against Boston from 1946 to 1987. The Canadiens won six of their record 23 Stanley Cup titles over the Bruins.

Things have evened out a bit since then. But the difference between the hard-nosed Bruins and the glamorous Canadiens has always been there. And the animosity between the two teams has only grown. After all,

There is no love lost between the Montreal Canadiens and the Boston Bruins.

no two NHL teams have played more—including the playoffs—than the Bruins and Canadiens.

Like a lot of hockey feuds, there has been plenty of bloodshed between these two teams. One famous incident was in 1955. The Bruins targeted Canadiens star Maurice Richard. That led to a fight that resulted in Richard punching a linesman who was trying to break it up. Boston police tried to arrest Richard in the locker room but were turned away. He was eventually suspended for the rest of the season. Fans in Montreal rioted in protest.

Almost exactly 56 years later, Bruins massive defenseman Zdeno Chara almost ran into trouble with Montreal police. He had checked Canadiens player Max Pacioretty into the metal post at the side of the players' bench. The hit ended Pacioretty's season. There was a criminal investigation, but it never led to an arrest. However, this was another violent chapter in this old rivalry.

BOSTON'S BEST

On the first two Mondays of each February, college hockey turns its attention to the Beanpot Tournament in Boston. It is played among the city's four major programs: Boston University, Boston College, Northeastern University, and Harvard University. The semifinals are played on the first Monday. The winners meet one week later for the title. The losers play for third place. The passion is intense. Boston University has dominated the event since it began in 1952. In 1978, hundreds of fans were stranded at the Boston Garden when a historic blizzard hit during the semifinals.

The Chicago Blackhawks' Patrick Kane attempts a shot against Detroit Red Wings goalie Jimmy Howard during a 2012 game.

Another Original Rivalry

In 1926, the Detroit Cougars beat the Chicago Black Hawks for the first win in team history. It also happened to be Chicago's first loss in team history. Thus began another great Original Six rivalry. The Cougars soon became the Red Wings. The Black Hawks became the Blackhawks. And the two teams have since played more than 700 times in the regular season. That is more than any other two teams.

The Montreal Canadiens and the Boston Bruins developed a fierce rivalry on the ice. The Canadiens' rivalry with the Toronto Maple Leafs is deeper than that. Montreal is in Quebec. It is the only Canadian province where French is the official language. That makes them very proud. People from Quebec see the Canadiens as ambassadors for French Canada. Games against other Canadian teams—especially Original Six rival Toronto—are always heated. Very often, the visiting team has as many fans in the arena as the home team.

Chicago and Detroit are two hard-nosed cities rich with sports tradition. Their hockey teams are no exception. Hall of Famers such as Gordie Howe, Alex Delvecchio, and Steve Yzerman have starred for Detroit over the years. For the Blackhawks it was stars such as Bobby Hull and Stan Mikita. Now Patrick Kane and Jonathan Toews are leading the way.

These two teams were the only Original Six teams from the Midwest. That helped build their rivalry into a regional one. Their ancient homes also helped. The Red Wings played in Olympia Stadium from 1927 to 1979. It is otherwise known as "The Old Red Barn." The Blackhawks called the famous Chicago Stadium home from 1929 to 1994. It was known as "The Madhouse on Madison." Both were intimidating buildings that fed the rivalry.

Border Battle

Women's hockey has a much shorter history than men's hockey. That short history is punctuated by important games played between the United States and Canada. The two countries share a border that is more than 5,000 miles (8,047 km) long. They also share a belief that theirs is the better team on the frozen pond.

The first Women's World Championship tournament was played in 1990. It was played 14 times through 2012. Each time Team USA and Canada met in the gold-medal game.

The most famous game in the rivalry was in 1998. Women's hockey debuted in the Olympic Winter Games that year. As expected, the United States and Canada met for the championship. However, the Americans upset the favored Canadians 3–1 to claim the first gold medal. Players such as Team USA's Cammi Granato and Canada's Hayley Wickenheiser became women's hockey legends that winter.

The rules limit checking in women's hockey. But games between the United States and Canada are always more physical than others. The intensity comes out each time they meet. In 2009, there was a rare brawl at the end of an exhibition game. In 2012 at the World Championship

RED WINGS–AVALANCHE

The Detroit Red Wings are one of the NHL's oldest teams. The Colorado Avalanche have only been around since 1995. Before that they were the Quebec Nordiques. But the Red Wings and Avalanche developed a strong rivalry as they often fought for the NHL's Western Conference crown during the mid-1990s. They combined to win five Stanley Cups over a seven-year span. Several future Hall of Fame players were on each team. And these great stars would not hesitate to fight. The most famous brawl took place in 1997. It included an all-time great goalie fight between Colorado's Patrick Roy and Detroit's Mike Vernon.

Team USA defenseman Angela Ruggiero skates with the American flag after beating Canada to win the Olympic gold medal in 1998.

GLOBAL SUPERPOWERS

The United States and the Soviet Union were rivals more in real life than in hockey in 1980. The two countries were global superpowers politically. On the hockey rink, however, the Soviets were simply the best. Plus, the United States brought a team of amateurs to the Olympic Winter Games that year in Lake Placid, New York. The Soviets had their full-strength team with professionals. In an exhibition game just before the Olympics, the Soviets beat Team USA 10–3. But when they met in the final round of the Olympics, the United States shocked the Soviets with a 4–3 victory. Americans who normally were not interested in hockey became glued to the game, which became known as the "Miracle on Ice." It did not necessarily matter the sport; the Americans simply defeating the favored Soviets was a massive event.

finals in Burlington, Vermont, the teams combined for 18 penalties in a very heated game.

US forward Kelli Stack summed up the rivalry after that meeting in Gutterson Fieldhouse.

"It was really rough out there, but to me, this is always how it goes with our games," Stack said. "Definitely, for us, our games against Canada will always be the most physical."

Chapter 5

GREAT SOCCER RIVALRIES

No sport matters more in Spain than soccer. And through the years, two teams have dominated the sport.

Madrid and Barcelona are the two largest cities in Spain. And Real Madrid and FC Barcelona are the two largest teams in those cities. In fact, many people who live in other cities still cheer for one of these teams. That has helped them both grow into global powers. When they play it is called "El Classico."

Like many soccer rivalries, though, this one goes deeper than the games. Barcelona is in a region called Catalonia. The people there have their own language. And many also have a desire to be independent from Spain. They rally around the soccer team to represent their cause. Meanwhile, Madrid is Spain's capital. In the early 1900s, Spain's king blessed the team. That allowed it to have a crown on the logo and

Barcelona's Lionel Messi, *left*, and Real Madrid's Cristiano Ronaldo, shown in 2012, are two of the best players in soccer history.

real (Spanish for "royal") in the name. Since it began in 1902, the rivalry has been defined by politics as much as the wins and losses.

The rivalry intensified in the 1950s when the clubs fought over Argentinian star Alfredo Di Stefano. Both sides claimed to sign him. Eventually, he went to Madrid. He helped Real Madrid win the first five European Cups. That tournament is now called the Champions League. Through 2012 no team had won more than Madrid's nine European titles.

Barcelona won for the first time in 1992. Then it won three between 2006 and 2011. A new Argentinean player named Lionel Messi played a key role in two of those wins.

The teams' success and history have drawn in fans from around the world. It was reported that more than 500 million people worldwide watched an El Classico match in 2002.

The Old Firm

Celtic and Rangers are the two biggest teams in Scotland. Both teams play in Scotland's largest city, Glasgow. And each team represents a different religion. Rangers are a club backed by Protestants. Celtic are supported by Catholics. That makes "Old Firm" games between the two teams very emotional. Sometimes they become violent.

In 1980, thousands of fans stormed from the stands after one tense match. They rioted on the field for several minutes. The Old Firm derby has also led to assaults and even deaths on the days when the two teams meet.

The Old Firm derby between Celtic, *left*, and Rangers is one of the most heated rivalries in the world.

The clubs began play in 1888. Ever since then, the series has been pretty even. In a given year it is almost certain one of these two teams will win the Scottish league. However, Rangers was punished in 2012 for having too much debt. The team was relegated to the fourth tier of Scottish soccer. That meant the two teams would—at least temporarily—play in different leagues.

MANCHESTER UNITED–LIVERPOOL

Soccer was invented in England. The English Premier League is one of the most famous professional sports leagues in the world. And no Premier League game is bigger than Liverpool and Manchester United. A distance of only approximately 30 miles (48.3 km) separates these two cities in northwest England. The two teams have been playing since 1894. Both claim to be the greatest English team ever. Liverpool's five European titles are the most of any English team. But Manchester United's 20 English championships were the most through 2013. For decades after 1964, not one player transferred from one team to the other.

USA-Mexico

Soccer has a long history in the United States and Mexico. But in the United States, the sport was very much in the background for several decades. That began to change in the 1990s. The United States began investing more in soccer. Millions of kids began playing the sport. Team USA even became a regular in the World Cup. The best team in North America, though? Not so fast.

The Mexican and US governments don't always agree. That tension carries over when the teams meet on the soccer field. And these two teams meet a lot.

Both are in a region called CONCACAF. It represents North America, Central America, and the Caribbean. Every two years CONCACAF has a championship tournament called the Gold Cup. Even more important is the World Cup. Countries must qualify for that tournament through their

The United States' Alexi Lalas goes down after being kneed during an altercation with Mexico players in 1997.

region. Multiple teams qualify from each region. But the games between the United States and Mexico are always intense.

Mexico often hosts them at Estadio Azteca in Mexico City. The huge stadium is hostile for visitors. The United States has never won a World Cup qualifier there. But the United States has its own home field advantage. In 2002 and 2010, the game was scheduled for the winter months. So Team USA hosted Mexico in chilly Columbus, Ohio. The Americans won both games.

The biggest game in this rivalry was in 2002. That year both countries qualified for the World Cup. Then they both qualified for the second

Istanbul is the largest city in Turkey. The city is separated by the Bosphorus, a stretch of water that connects the Black Sea and the Mediterranean Sea. The Bosphorus also separates Europe and Asia. Fenerbahce was founded on the Asian side of the water. Galatasaray was founded on the European side. So while these two teams play on different continents, they play for city and country pride. Because of this natural divide, the fans are at each other as much as in any other rivalry. There has been plenty of violence over the years. These clubs also field teams in other sports as well, such as basketball.

round of the World Cup. As luck had it, they had to play each other in the round of 16. In a stunning victory, Team USA won 2–0. The win signaled that Mexico was no longer the undisputed king of CONCACAF.

Brazil-Argentina

The South American rivalry between neighbors Argentina and Brazil is based purely on the sport. It has produced many of the greatest figures in soccer history. Pele, Ronaldo, and Ronaldinho have played for Brazil. Di Stefano, Diego Maradona, and Messi have played for Argentina. The rivalry has also featured many great teams. From 1958 through 2002, seven of 12 World Cup titles went to either Brazil or Argentina.

This feud began in 1914, well before the first World Cup in 1930. However, neither country was a soccer power early on. Brazil did not win its first World Cup until 1958. Behind Pele and an exciting, offense-first strategy, Brazil won two more in 1962 and 1970. Argentina won its

Galatasaray, *left*, and Fenerbahce play in the same city but different continents.

first World Cup on home soil in 1978. However, fans most remember Argentina's 1986 win. That year Maradona dazzled fans with his dribbling and goal scoring. Many fans today still debate who was the best player ever: Pele or Maradona.

Chapter 6

GREAT INDIVIDUAL RIVALRIES

Muhammad Ali was a showman. Joe Frazier was stoic but powerful. And when the two got into the ring together, boxing fans saw some of the best bouts ever.

The two heavyweights met three times. Their 1971 fight at Madison Square Garden in New York City was the biggest. It was an amazing extravaganza. Ali and Frazier were two of the most famous athletes in the United States. And both came into the bout undefeated. Frazier was the heavyweight champion. But Ali had been the champion. He lost the title without losing a bout due to his refusal to fight in the Vietnam War.

The hype leading into the bout was immense. Ali taunted Frazier and called him names. But Frazier proved himself in the ring. The two slugged it out for 15 rounds. Finally, in the fifteenth round, Frazier knocked Ali down with a powerful left hook. Ali got up, but at the end of the round

Joe Frazier, *left*, hits Muhammad Ali during the fifteenth round of their 1971 fight in New York City.

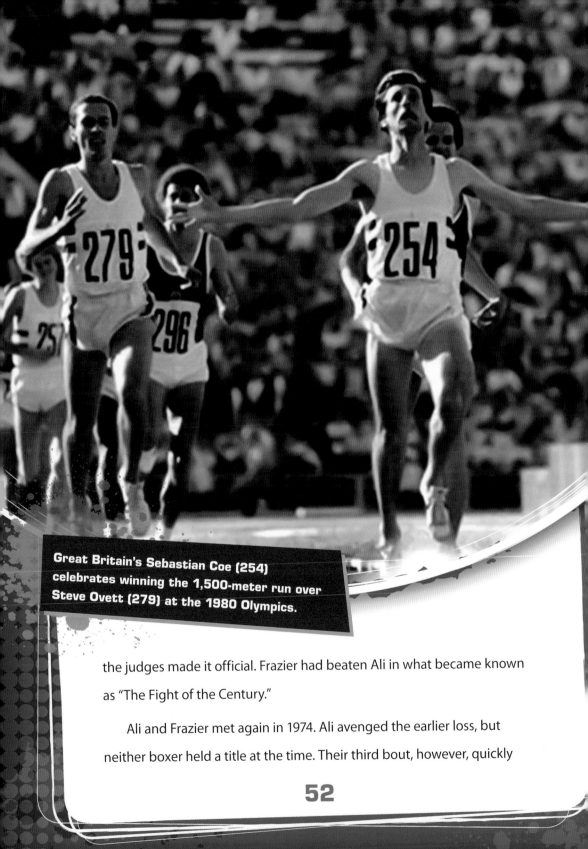

Great Britain's Sebastian Coe (254) celebrates winning the 1,500-meter run over Steve Ovett (279) at the 1980 Olympics.

the judges made it official. Frazier had beaten Ali in what became known as "The Fight of the Century."

Ali and Frazier met again in 1974. Ali avenged the earlier loss, but neither boxer held a title at the time. Their third bout, however, quickly became legendary. Ali came into the fight as the heavyweight champion. Leading up to the fight, he took every opportunity he had to insult Frazier. Ali called Frazier a "gorilla" and "stupid."

Frazier did his best to ignore the insults. In the ring, he nearly fought Ali to the end. But before the fifteenth round began, Frazier's trainer stopped the fight. The boxer's left eye was swollen shut. The bout became known as the "Thrilla in Manila," as it took place in Manila, Philippines.

The three Ali-Frazier bouts went down as some of the most famous in history. However, they were also brutal. Ali said he was "next to death" at the end of the 1975 fight.

Long after their brutal wars came to an end, Ali and Frazier chose to remain rivals. Ali had said many mean things about Frazier during their careers. Frazier always seemed to hold a grudge toward Ali. However, some people claim the two boxers made up prior to Frazier's death in 2011.

COE VS. OVETT

Two middle-distance runners from England were on the biggest stage at the 1980 Olympic Games in Moscow, Russia. Sebastian Coe was the favorite to win the 800 meters. Steve Ovett had not lost in the 1,500 meters for more than two years. Amazingly, Ovett came from behind to defeat Coe in the 800 meters. Coe had almost a week to think about that loss. Then he upset Ovett in the 1,500 in one of the great runs in Olympics history. If you were a fan of distance running, or just a citizen in England at the time, you rooted for either Coe or Ovett.

Jack Nicklaus, *left*, helps Arnold Palmer slip into his green jacket as the winner of the 1964 Masters.

Golfing Greats

Great rivalries take their sport to new levels in popularity. That is what Arnold Palmer and Jack Nicklaus did in the 1960s. Golf became more televised during that era. So all of the new fans sat on their couches at home and could pick a side—Arnie or Jack.

Early on, most people chose Palmer. He was handsome. He had a swagger. He flew his own planes. He was a true American. Palmer's loud supporters were called "Arnie's Army."

Meanwhile, Nicklaus was made fun of for being a little chubby. He played very slowly. That frustrated other golfers, including Palmer. Nicklaus was focused on the course. But he could really play golf. Together, the two would fight for golf supremacy throughout the 1960s.

The rivalry really took off when 22-year-old Nicklaus beat Palmer by one stroke in the 1962 US Open. The event was played at the Oakmont Country Club in western Pennsylvania. That was Palmer country, and his fans really let Nicklaus know it. But Nicklaus was not bothered that almost everyone was rooting for his rival. Nicklaus defeated Palmer in a playoff for his first win in a major.

At the time, the two were not friendly. By the time Palmer outlasted Nicklaus in the 1973 Bob Hope Classic for his last tour victory, they had formed a bond. After all, these were two of the greatest competitors in all of sports, and they helped make golf what it is today.

Racquet Rivals

From 1973 to 1988, Chris Evert and Martina Navratilova played 80 times on the tennis court. Sixty of those meetings were in the finals of tournaments. Fourteen of those finals were in Grand Slam events. If one was in the spotlight, chances are the other was right alongside her. Evert and Navratilova helped redefine women's athletics. They paved the way for players such as Steffi Graf, Monica Seles, and Venus and Serena Williams to make millions of dollars.

What made this rivalry so unique was the friendship that Evert and Navratilova had. They had many differences. Evert was the all-American girl. Navratilova was from Czechoslovakia but later represented the United States. On the court, no player had more desire to defeat Evert than Navratilova. Navratilova often showed her emotion on and off the court. Evert, known as the "Ice Maiden," did not.

However, they put their differences aside off the court. They often teamed up as doubles partners. And through each of their 80 matches, there was great respect. Both women won 18 Grand Slam singles titles. Navratilova won 1,442 singles matches, more than anyone in tennis history. Evert still had the record for the best all-time winning percentage

FEDERER-NADAL

For 211 straight weeks between 2005 and 2009, Roger Federer and Rafael Nadal were the number one and number two ranked tennis players in the world. From 2006 to 2008 they met in all six French Open and Wimbledon finals. Nobody could challenge Nadal and Federer. Their greatest match came in the 2008 Wimbledon final. The match lasted almost five hours before Nadal won. It was the longest final in Wimbledon history and many said it was as good, or even better, than the famous John McEnroe-Bjorn Borg 1980 final.

Chris Evert, *left*, and Martina Navratilova joke with a police officer at Wimbledon in 1985. The two players later met in the final.

through 2012. And they formed perhaps the strongest bond of any rivals that ever played the sport.

McEnroe and Borg

Bjorn Borg and John McEnroe dominated men's tennis during the 1970s and 1980s. Their 1980 match for the Wimbledon championship went down as one of the greatest tennis matches ever.

McEnroe was the cocky, loud American trying to knock Borg off his throne. Borg, the quiet, focused Swede, had won the last four Wimbledon titles. His attempt at a fifth straight championship would become the ultimate battle.

They played for nearly four hours. McEnroe stayed alive by winning a classic fourth-set tiebreaker. But Borg triumphed in the fifth set and took home the crown once again. McEnroe finally ended Borg's Wimbledon streak in the 1981 final.

McEnroe and Borg met just 14 times. Both of them won seven times. By contrast, 1960s stars Rod Laver and Ken Rosewall faced off 141 times. But the intensity of the Borg-McEnroe matchups, as well as their very different styles, made them perfect rivals. Their different styles even showed in retirement. McEnroe has remained outspoken and in the spotlight as a television commentator. Borg chose to live a quiet life in retirement. Eventually, like many rivals who gain respect for one another, they became good friends.

★ There are two soccer teams in Milan, Italy. They are two of the biggest club teams in the world. And both share the same San Siro stadium. But AC Milan and Inter Milan are two of the biggest rivals in sports. They started as one club in 1899 called the Milan Cricket and Football Club. However, one group broke away in 1908 because it wanted to sign international players as well as Italian players. It became known as Inter Milan. The other club later became known as AC Milan. Games between the two teams are known as *Derby della Madonnina*.

★ Williams College and Amherst College have played football against each other since 1884. This Western Massachusetts rivalry is called "The Biggest Little Game in America."

★ The University of Kansas and the University of Missouri long had a rivalry known as "The Border War." These two states' disdain for each other dates to the Civil War. However, the rivalry took a hiatus in 2012 when Missouri moved to the Southeastern Conference.

★ As far as swimming goes, two countries have traditionally dominated: Australia and the United States. These two countries have dominated in the pool ever since Johnny Weissmuller led the Americans over the Aussies in the 800-meter relay in the 1924 Olympic Games. In more recent times, swimmers such as Australians Ian "Thorpedo" Thorpe and Leisel Jones and Americans Michael Phelps, Ryan Lochte, and Natalie Coughlin have kept the rivalry as relevant as ever.

GLOSSARY

ACE
The best pitcher on a given baseball team.

ALL-AROUND PLAYER
An athlete who is good at all portions of his/her sport.

ALUMNUS
A graduate of a given school.

AVENGED
Made up for a previous wrongdoing.

DERBY
A term for a regular soccer series between two teams from the same area.

EXHIBITION
A game played for entertainment and practice but with a result that does not count in the standings.

GRAND SLAM
The four major tournaments in golf and tennis.

MIDDLE-DISTANCE
Running events that are longer than sprints but no longer than 1,500 meters.

PENNANT
A long, triangular flag. In baseball, the word is used to describe a league championship.

POWERHOUSE
A team in any sport that is very good.

RELEGATED
Sent down to a lower division. In international soccer, many leagues are interconnected so teams bounce between divisions based upon their success.

WINNING PERCENTAGE
The percent of games a player or team wins.

FOR MORE INFORMATION

Selected Bibliography

Corbett, Bernard M., and Paul Simpson. *The Only Game That Matters: The Harvard/ Yale Rivalry*. New York: Crown Publishers, 2004.

Howard, Johnette. *The Rivals: Chris Evert vs. Martina Navratilova, Their Epic Duels and Extraordinary Friendship*. New York: Broadway Books, 2005.

Rosenberg, Michael. *War as They Knew it: Woody Hayes, Bo Schembechler, and America in a Time of Unrest*. New York: Grand Central Publishing, 2008.

Wendel, Tim. *Going for the Gold: How the U.S. Won at Lake Placid*. Westport, CT: Lawrence Hill & Company, 1980.

Wojciechowski, Gene. *Cubs Nation: 162 Games, 162 Stories, 1 Addiction*. New York: Doubleday, 2005.

Further Readings

Chansky, Art. *Blue Blood: Duke-Carolina: Inside the Most Storied Rivalry in College Hoops*. New York: St. Martin's Griffin, 2006.

Cronin, Matthew. *Epic: John McEnroe, Bjorn Borg and the Greatest Tennis Season Ever*. Hoboken, NJ: Wiley, 2011.

Kahn, Roger. *The Era, 1947-1957: When the Yankees, Giants and the Dodgers Ruled the World*. Lincoln, NE: Bison Books, 2002.

Rappoport, Ken, and Barry Wilner. *Football Feuds: The Greatest College Football Rivalries*. Guilford, CT: Lyons Press, 2007.

Vaccaro, Mike. *Emperors and Idiots: The Hundred Year Rivalry Between the Yankees and Red Sox, From the Very Beginning to the End of the Curse*. New York: Broadway Books, 2006.

Web Links

To learn more about the biggest rivalries in sports, visit ABDO Publishing Company online at **www.abdopublishing.com**. Web sites about the biggest rivalries in sports are featured on our Book Links page. These links are routinely monitored and updated to provide the most current information available.

Places to Visit

Naismith Memorial Basketball Hall of Fame
1000 Hall Fame Ave
Springfield, MA 01105
(413) 781-6500
www.hoophall.com
The Naismith Memorial Basketball Hall of Fame honors basketball's greatest players and moments.

National Baseball Hall of Fame and Museum
25 Main Street
Cooperstown, NY 13326
(888) 425-5633
www.baseballhall.org
This hall of fame and museum highlights the greatest players and moments in the history of baseball.

Pro Football Hall of Fame
2121 George Halas Drive NW
Canton, OH 44708
(330) 456-8207
www.profootballhof.com
This hall of fame and museum highlights the greatest players and moments in the history of the NFL.

INDEX

About the Author

Tony Lee is a sportswriter based in Boston. He completed his undergraduate studies at the University of Vermont and his graduate work at Emerson College. He served as a writer and editor covering all sports at ESPN and later as the Boston Red Sox beat writer for the New England Sports Network. Lee has covered the Red Sox, Celtics, Bruins, and Patriots for a variety of outlets, including ESPNBoston.com and the *Metro Boston*. He lives with his wife and son.